J N-F 778.9979 Hamilton
21.95
3/2019

WITHDRAWN

Hesston Public Library
P.O. Box 640
300 North Main
Hesston, KS 67062

DIGITAL PHOTOGRAPHY

SPORTS PHOTOGRAPHY

By John Hamilton

Abdo & Daughters
An imprint of Abdo Publishing | abdopublishing.com

abdopublishing.com

Published by Abdo Publishing, a division of ABDO, PO Box 398166, Minneapolis, Minnesota 55439. Copyright © 2019 by Abdo Consulting Group, Inc. International copyrights reserved in all countries. No part of this book may be reproduced in any form without written permission from the publisher. Abdo & Daughters™ is a trademark and logo of Abdo Publishing.

Printed in the United States of America, North Mankato, Minnesota.
072018
092018

Editor: Sue Hamilton
Copy Editor: Bridget O'Brien
Graphic Design: Sue Hamilton
Cover Design: Candice Keimig and Pakou Moua
Cover Photos: iStock
Interior Images: AP-pgs 4-5, 23 (top) & 38; Eastman-Kodak-pg 6 (top); Fujifilm North America-pg 11; Getty-pgs 33, 34 & 39; GoPro-pg 12 (top & bottom); iStock-pgs 9 (top), 13, 15 (top & bottom), 18 (top), 19, 20 (top), 21 (bottom), 22, 24 (top & bottom), 26, 27, 28, 29, 31, 35, 37, 40, 41, 44 & 45 (top); John Hamilton-pgs 14, 18 (bottom), 32, 42 & 43; Nikon USA-pgs 7 (inset), 8, 14 (inset), 15 (inset), 16 (inset), 17 (inset) & 20 (bottom); Science Source-pg 36; Shutterstock-pgs 6 (bottom), 7, 9 (bottom) 10, 16, 17 (top & bottom), 21 (top), 23 (bottom), 25 & 30; U.S. Copyright Office-pg 45 (bottom).

Library of Congress Control Number: 2017963904
Publisher's Cataloging-in-Publication Data
Names: Hamilton, John, author.
Title: Sports photography / by John Hamilton.
Description: Minneapolis, Minnesota : Abdo Publishing, 2019. | Series: Digital photography | Includes online resources and index.
Identifiers: ISBN 9781532115905 (lib.bdg.) | ISBN 9781532156830 (ebook)
Subjects: LCSH: Photography of sports--Juvenile literature. | Photography of team sports--Juvenile literature. | Sports journalism--Juvenile literature. | Photography--Digital techniques--Juvenile literature.
Classification: DDC 778.9979--dc23

CONTENTS

The Thrill of Action Sports 4

Cameras 6

Action Cameras 12

Lenses 14

Exposure 18

Getting A Steady Shot 22

Know Your Sport 26

Composition 28

Try Different Angles 30

Look For Emotion 32

Don't Chimp 34

Panning to Show Motion 36

Shooting Details 38

Cropping 40

The Digital Darkroom 42

Backing Up Your Photos 44

Glossary 46

Online Resources 47

Index 48

THE THRILL OF ACTION SPORTS

Shooting sports can be difficult even for experienced photographers. Not only do you need the right kind of camera gear to get superior shots, you have to know it inside and out. You also have to know about the sport you're shooting. That helps you predict when and where the best action will happen.

Despite the challenges, it is a thrill to shoot fast-moving sporting events. Freezing a split-second of time helps us see action that is too fast for the naked eye. Good photography helps us appreciate human drama, whether the sport is football, hockey, soccer, or dozens of other competitions.

CAPTURING PEAK ACTION

One of the most challenging parts of sports photography is anticipating when the best, or "peak," action will occur. These dramatic moments are captured successfully by having knowledge of the sport, using the right photographic equipment, being at the right place at the right time, and sometimes having just a little bit of luck. Practice makes any skill better, and that is especially true of sports photography.

CAMERAS

Digital photography captures a scene when light passes through a lens and is focused onto an image sensor. The sensor converts the light into digital form. It is then stored as a file that can be transferred to a computer for later processing. The first portable digital camera was made by Eastman Kodak in 1975. It weighed eight pounds (3.6 kg) and shot only in black-and-white. Digital cameras as we know them today first became popular in the 1990s and early 2000s.

The first portable digital camera was made by Steven Sasson for Eastman Kodak in 1975.

Most sports photographers have long given up film because of the big advantages of digital. Being able to see your photos right away lets you change settings if needed. Another advantage is the hundreds of shots you can take on a single memory card, eliminating the chance of missing a shot while changing a 36-shot film cartridge.

Many modern digital cameras are lightweight and easy to hold.

With a DSLR (Digital Single Lens Reflex) camera, you can look through the viewfinder or use the camera's screen display to see exactly what you're shooting.

Most professional sports photographers today use DSLR (Digital Single Lens Reflex) cameras. With a DSLR, you actually peer through the camera lens so you can see exactly what you're shooting. Angle of view and sharpness are determined by the lens. DSLR lenses are "interchangeable," which means you can swap out one lens for another depending on your creative needs.

Once light travels inside a DSLR, it is diverted by a mirror into a glass prism, which directs the light into the viewfinder. When you press the shutter release button, the "reflex" mirror flips up and the shutter behind it opens. Light strikes the image processor. After the exposure, the shutter closes, and the mirror flips back down.

The camera's image sensor has millions of light-capturing pixels that record an image. The greater the number of pixels, the higher the resolution of the picture. A 20-megapixel (20-million-pixel) sensor almost always has a better resolution than a 10-megapixel sensor. Modern DSLR sensors usually have at least 16 to 24 megapixels. The size of the image sensor is also important. The large sensors in many DSLRs produce the most detailed pictures, and they can capture images in low light without too much digital noise ruining the scene. Another advantage for sports photographers is that you can crop creatively, using just part of the frame, and the quality will still be acceptable.

The inside workings of a DSLR camera.

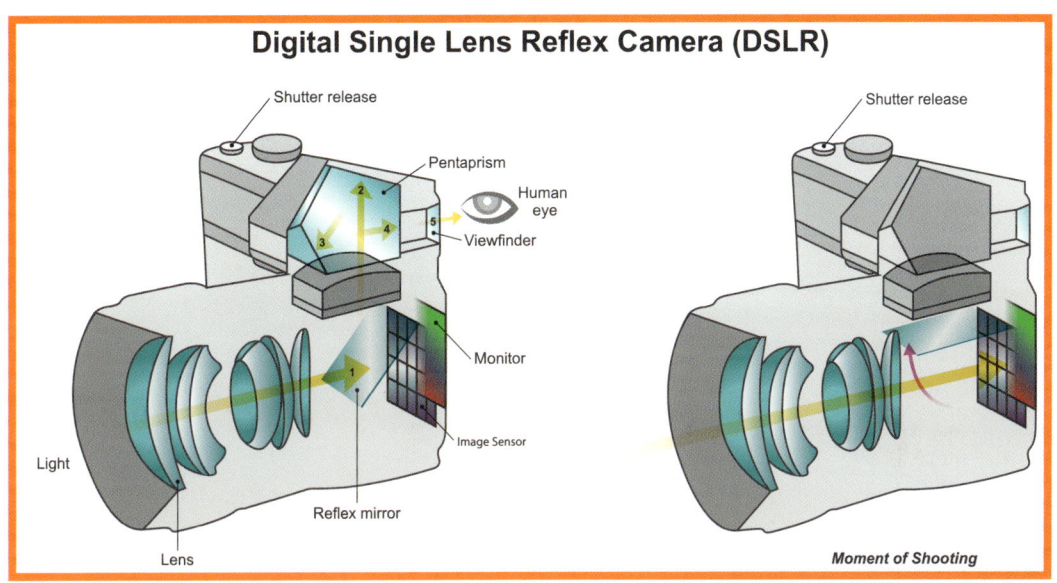

This diagram shows how a DSLR camera creates a photograph.

8 TIPS FOR CARING FOR YOUR CAMERA

1. Use an air blower and microfiber cloth to clean your camera regularly.
2. Use a strap when carrying your camera.
3. When not in use, keep the camera safe in a bag or case.
4. Many photographers put a UV or skylight filter on the front of their lenses. These block ultraviolet rays from the Sun (which degrade image quality) and protect your expensive lenses from dust or scratches.
5. Make sure you always have spare batteries.
6. Keep your camera out of the rain.
7. Keep your camera out of hot cars.
8. Never leave your camera unattended.

Cell phones are commonly used as both a primary and a backup camera. Most cell phones have a complicated lens arrangement. This has helped improve their photo quality greatly in recent years.

There is an old saying that the best camera is the one you have on you. For many people, that means a cell phone. The image quality of most cell phones has greatly improved in recent years. Most professional photographers carry one as a backup in case their DSLRs are not handy when a photo opportunity arises. Cell phones do the focusing and adjust exposure for you. There are clip-on lenses that allow you to shoot wide-angle or telephoto images.

Serious sports photographers do not use cell phone cameras. They use DSLRs. It is harder to control shutter speeds and depth of field with cell phones. They do not usually perform as well in low-light situations, such as inside dimly lit gymnasiums. Most also cannot take a rapid series of shots. Some newer cameras have "burst mode" that can do this, but their performance does not yet match that of a DSLR.

Mirrorless cameras are becoming more popular each year. Like DSLRs, different lenses can be mounted on most of them (some have fixed lenses). However, there is no mirror or glass prism. This makes mirrorless cameras lightweight and quiet to shoot. Yet, they have excellent image quality, even in low light.

If you are a beginner, don't worry too much about which camera to buy. Think about what you want to do with it and which features are important to you. Amazing images can be taken with almost all digital cameras sold today. Their quality gets better each year. The truth is, it's the eye (and the mind) behind the camera that matters most. Creative photographers can make world-class images no matter what they're shooting with.

A mirrorless camera produced by Fujifilm. This type of camera is lightweight and quiet to shoot, yet produces excellent image quality, even in low light.

ACTION CAMERAS

In recent years, small cameras in protective shells have become very popular. They are used to shoot action-packed outdoor sports such as surfing, skateboarding, motocross, and many others. The cameras are built rugged and lightweight so that they can actually be a part of the action. They are often mounted to handlebars, helmets, or sticks that are held in front of athletes as they perform.

A mountable GoPro camera.

A handlebar-mounted GoPro allows athletes to take action shots as they move.

A "you-are-there" surfing photo created with an action camera.

The "you-are-there" images that are made by action cameras are possible because of wide-angle views, waterproof cases, and a rugged build. Getting knocked around or dunked in the ocean doesn't faze these little powerhouses. It would be very difficult to use a DSLR in such a freewheeling way.

Action cameras are made by many companies. GoPro is by far the most familiar, but these cameras are also manufactured by Sony, Garmin, Olympus, and others.

LENSES

Just as important as your camera are the lenses you use. They determine the "field of view" of your scene. A wide-angle lens shows more of the surrounding area. A telephoto captures just a small part, which is why everything looks magnified.

A lens's field of view is measured in millimeters. A "normal" field of view captured by a full-frame image sensor is about 50mm. That is about the same as what you perceive with your eyes. Common wide-angle lenses are about 24mm to 35mm. Super-wide lenses start at about 10mm. Below that are fisheye lenses, which are used for special effects because of their distortion.

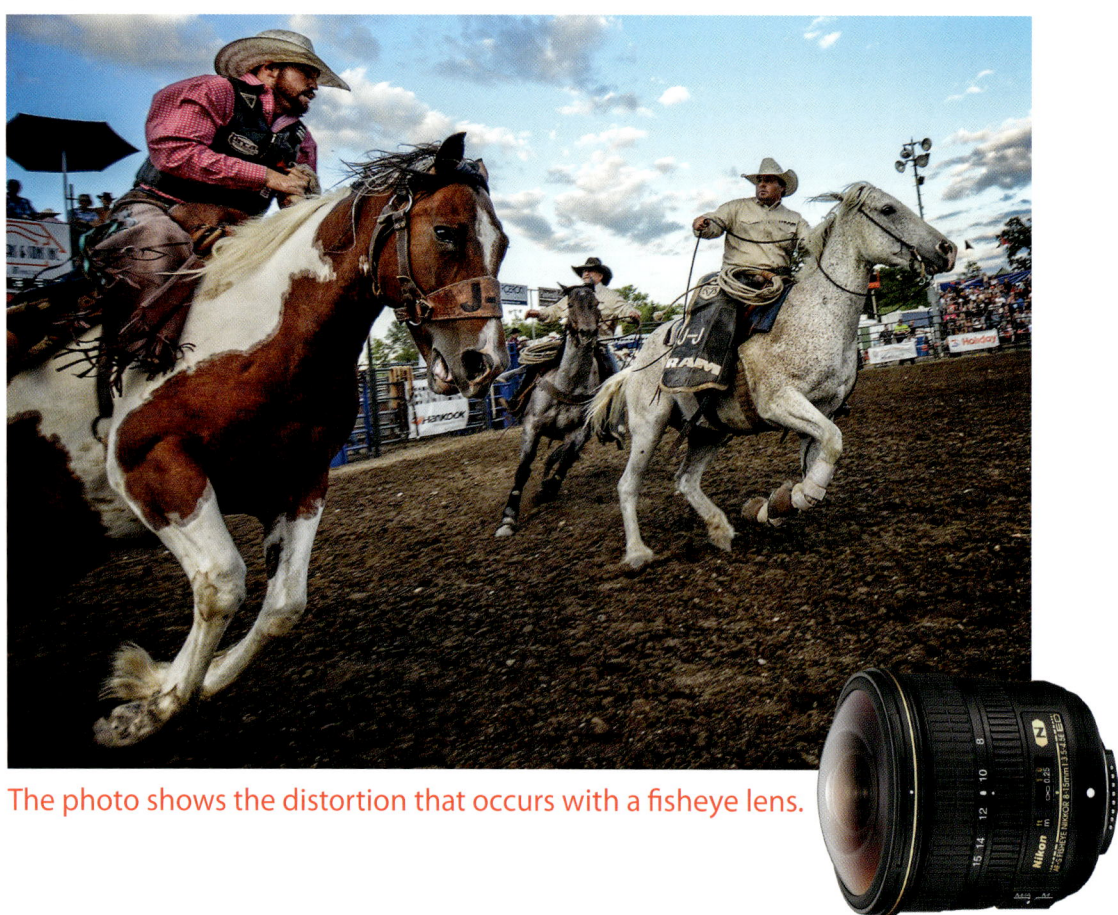

The photo shows the distortion that occurs with a fisheye lens.

A wide-angle lens captures much of the surrounding area.

Most sports photographers own at least one wide-angle lens. They make it possible to capture a whole scene, such as a stadium. They are also handy when a subject moves very close to you. Wide-angle lenses work well in low light. They also have a big range of focus, or "depth of field." That makes it easy to keep everything in sharp focus, from a foreground football on the ground to a background goalpost.

FILTERS

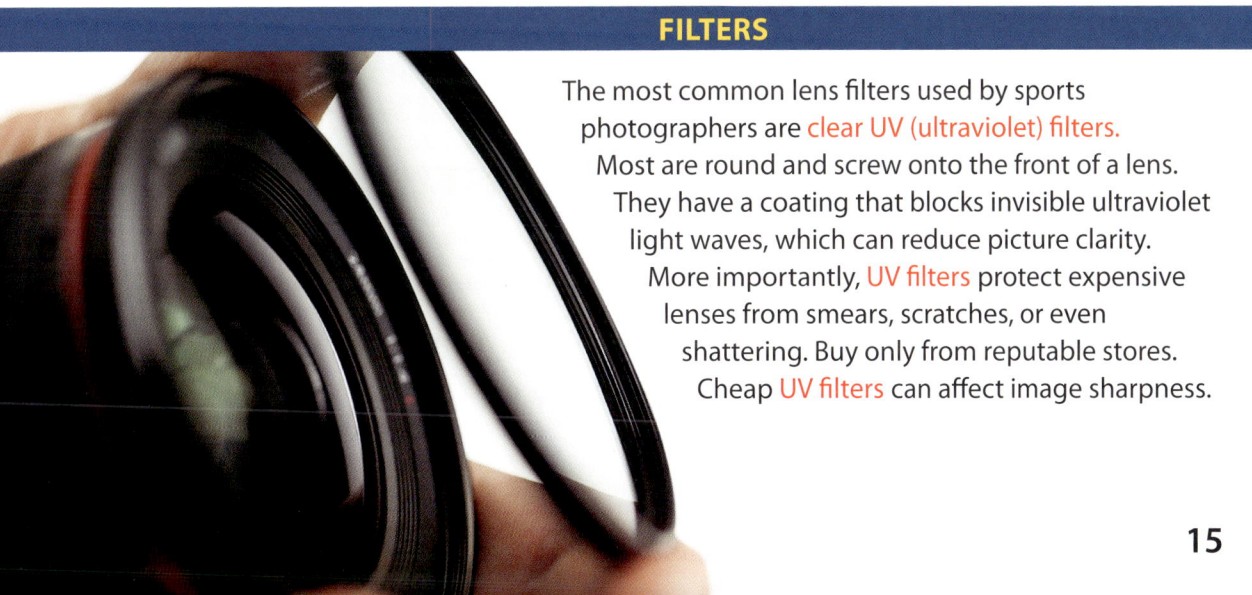

The most common lens filters used by sports photographers are clear UV (ultraviolet) filters. Most are round and screw onto the front of a lens. They have a coating that blocks invisible ultraviolet light waves, which can reduce picture clarity. More importantly, UV filters protect expensive lenses from smears, scratches, or even shattering. Buy only from reputable stores. Cheap UV filters can affect image sharpness.

Telephoto lenses help fill the frame with your subject even when you're on the sidelines.

    Telephotos are the workhorse lenses of most sports photographers. Their angle of view is very narrow. This creates a "reach" that makes it seem like you're in the middle of the action. To get pro-quality sports shots from the sidelines, you need a zoom lens with a focal range of about 80-200mm. These lenses can be used in many fast-moving situations.

    Above 200mm, telephoto lenses are very expensive, usually several thousand dollars. "Big glass" ranges from about 300mm to 600mm or higher. One reason they are so expensive is that pro-quality lenses are "fast." They have large maximum apertures, usually from f/2.8 to f/4, that let in the most light. That helps freeze action with good sharpness.

A teleconverter attached to a lens is a fairly inexpensive way to get even closer to the action.

One way to get the massive reach of a pro-level telephoto without paying so much is to use a teleconverter that attaches to your existing lens. It can increase the focal length of your lens (usually multiplied 1.4 to 2 times) with a small loss of quality, for a fraction of the cost.

LENS HOODS

Lens Hood

Lens hoods are plastic extensions that fit onto the front of your lens. They keep Sun flare from washing out your photos. They can also protect your expensive lens's front glass element from bumps and scratches.

EXPOSURE

A camera's shutter-speed dial.

Exposure is the amount of light that strikes the camera's image sensor. Three settings determine the "correct" exposure. They include ISO, shutter speed, and aperture. All three work together.

ISO is the image sensor's sensitivity to light. If you double the ISO, you make the sensor twice as sensitive. However, more digital noise is then created. The lower the ISO, the better the quality. For example, when shooting in bright sunlight, you would normally set an ISO of 100 or 200. However, in dim scenes, you might increase it to 800. Otherwise, your exposures would be so long that you couldn't hold your camera steady enough to avoid blurring (camera shake). Subject movement, especially when shooting sports, can also cause blurring during long exposures.

The center box, part of the main photo, shows digital noise because of a high ISO setting. The camera ISO was set to 1,600 because of dim lighting in a domed stadium.

Choosing the right exposure for a sports scene is a balance between areas of light and dark (tone) and focus (depth of field). These are controlled by shutter speed and aperture.

Shutter speed is the length of time the camera's shutter opens to let light strike the image sensor. It is measured in seconds (usually a fraction of a second). Each setting is twice as long, or half as short, as the setting next to it. Shutter speeds must be fairly fast to avoid camera shake, usually in the range of 1/125 to 1/250 second. Wide-angle lenses can be used with slower shutter speeds.

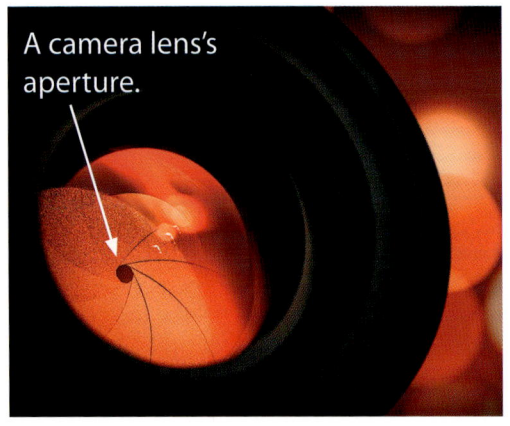

A camera lens's aperture.

Lenses have apertures, or holes, in the back where they are mounted to the camera. Apertures can be adjusted much like the irises in your eyes. They are measured in "f-stops." The smaller the f-stop number, the more light is allowed into the camera.

The important thing to remember is that if you increase one setting, such as shutter speed, then you must reduce the other setting (aperture) in order to get back to your original exposure.

When you are starting out, it's okay to put your camera on automatic. DSLRs have a setting on the exposure dial called "P," which stands for program mode. Modern cameras are like small computers. They examine the scene and figure out the math for you. The camera will pick a shutter speed and aperture combination. This will allow you to concentrate on other things, like focus and composition.

The exposure dial is set at "P" for program mode.

The small, or "shallow," depth of field in this photo ensures that only the pitcher is sharp, while the distracting background crowd is blurred.

As you get more practice taking pictures, you'll soon want to control these settings yourself in creative ways. For example, controlling the aperture also controls the amount of depth of field in your scene. That means you have more control over what is in sharp focus.

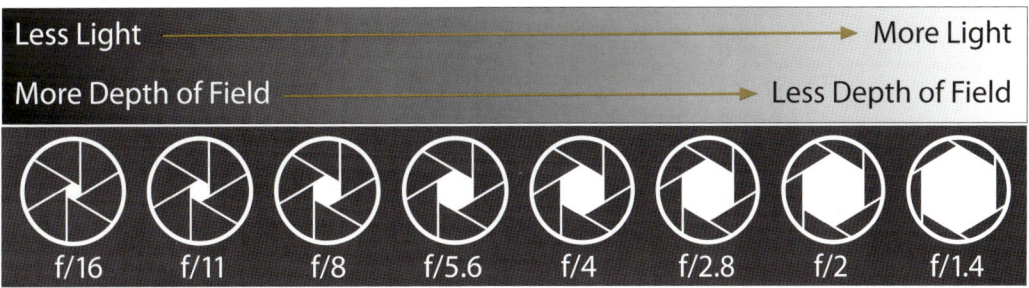

Typical lens f-stop settings.

GETTING A STEADY SHOT

Many sports photographers handhold their cameras while shooting. Bulky tripods are not practical, especially when moving up and down the sidelines to capture fast-moving action. To shoot without a tripod, hold your camera with your elbows tucked in near your body. The camera or telephoto lens should rest in the palm of your hand.

The trouble with not using a support, however, is the danger of camera shake. A photographer's hands shake slightly while holding the camera, especially with a big telephoto lens attached. These tiny movements happen several times per second. They cause the subject to appear jumpy in the viewfinder.

A steady hand and a fast shutter speed help capture the start of a swim race.

The camera shake effect gets worse as the focal length of the telephoto lens gets higher. It is much more difficult to handhold a 600mm lens than a 200mm lens. When the camera shutter opens, the shaky subject moves across the image sensor a tiny bit during the exposure. This is a common cause of blurry pictures. Camera shake might make the difference between having a mere snapshot and capturing an image good enough to be published.

To help freeze the action, photographers try to use shutter speeds of 1/1,000 second or less. With such fast shutter speeds, blur caused by handholding the camera is mostly eliminated.

BEST SHUTTER SPEED FOR HANDHOLDING THE CAMERA

If you're handholding your camera, how do you know if the shutter speed is fast enough to create a sharp image? The rule of thumb is to shoot at a shutter speed higher than the reciprocal of the focal length of your lens. In other words, if you're shooting with a 200mm lens, you'll need a shutter speed of at least 1/200 second in order to get a sharp picture. If you're shooting with a wide-angle 24mm lens, you can go all the way down to 1/24 second. If you set your camera to "Program" or "Auto," it will calculate this for you.

Vibration reduction (VR), or image stabilization, is often activated by a switch on the lens barrel. This advanced technology often helps produce sharper images.

To combat camera shake, some lenses come with a feature called vibration reduction, or image stabilization. They contain tiny sensors that detect motion. Elements inside the lens move in the opposite direction of the motion, which cancels out much of the blurriness. Some cameras have vibration reduction built into their bodies. When shake is detected, the image sensor itself moves to cancel out the blur. This technology often makes it possible to shoot in dim lighting conditions.

RAISE YOUR ISO

You're shooting with your lens wide open, perhaps at f/2.8. But your shutter speed is still too slow to capture action. Now what? Don't be afraid to raise your ISO, the image sensor's sensitivity to light. Crank it up, perhaps as high as ISO 1,600 or more, so that your shutter speed is at least 1/1,000 second. You will see more digital noise in your photos, but that is better than missing the shot. Also, modern DSLRs work remarkably well even at high ISOs.

A sports photographer uses a monopod to help steady and support his camera.

Even though vibration-reduction lenses help tremendously, there are situations where sports photographers need physical support. On very cloudy days, at night, or when shooting in badly lit gymnasiums, there may not be enough light to successfully handhold a camera. Also, long telephoto lenses (300mm and up) can be very heavy. A photographer's arms might get too tired to hold the camera steady.

In these situations, many sports photographers use monopods. These metal or carbon fiber supports are a compromise between handholding a camera and using a bulky tripod. If you have to reposition yourself during a fast-paced match, it is much easier to do so with a monopod. Also, monopods make it easier to access a second camera body with a wide-angle lens attached. You may have it hanging around your neck as a backup for when the action gets too close to shoot with a telephoto.

KNOW YOUR SPORT

To shoot sports, you must have more than technical skills and the right equipment. You also need to understand the sport that you are photographing. You have to anticipate where the peak action is going to happen and have your camera ready.

Don't stay in one place. Sometimes you have to move around to find interesting angles and different kinds of action. Go to team practices if you can. Observe how the players move and learn their habits. When game day comes, you'll be prepared to follow the action.

Sometimes you have to keep both eyes open as you get ready to shoot. One eye peers through the viewfinder, while you also watch for activity that might bring action into the frame. For example, if you're tightly focused on a baseball batter, you need to know when the pitcher has thrown the ball. Otherwise, by the time the ball crosses home plate, you won't react in time to catch the swing of the bat.

BURST MODE

Even if you know exactly when and where peak action will occur, it can be hard to capture that winning moment. Most sports photographers use their cameras' burst mode setting. Also called continuous shooting mode, it rapidly takes photos as long as the shutter release button is pressed. Some cheaper cameras take only two or three frames per second (fps), while professional cameras can shoot 10 fps or more.

COMPOSITION

Even though sports photography is mainly about capturing exciting drama that happens in a fraction of a second, creative composition is also important, just like in any other kind of photography. You don't need fancy equipment or exotic locations to make a stunning, well-composed image. Composition is all about arranging the scene in your viewfinder in the best way to tell your story.

Good composition uses color, contrast, texture, framing, and natural lines. All of these elements lead the viewer's eye to your subject. The best way to reduce clutter in your scene is to fill the frame with your subject and the design elements as much as possible. Be aware of empty space around your subject and get closer if you can.

Backgrounds can help or hurt your composition. Sometimes a busy background will give context to your scene. Other times, it distracts from your subject. Before taking a photo, check to be sure things like poles or pillars aren't growing out of the head of your subjects. Wide-open apertures, such as f/2.8 on some lenses, will blur the background, hiding much of the clutter.

THE RULE OF THIRDS

The "rule of thirds" is a way of dividing the viewfinder into sections and arranging your subject within the lines. Divide your viewfinder into three horizontal parts, and three vertical parts. Put your subject roughly near one of the intersecting lines. Don't always place your subjects in the center of the frame. Instead of a "rule," think of it as a helpful guideline. As you grow as a photographer, you will discover other ways to arrange elements in your frame that are interesting and tell a story.

TRY DIFFERENT ANGLES

When shooting sports, don't always stand and take pictures at eye level. To make your photos more interesting, try different angles. Many photographers get down on their knees during games to shoot upward. This creates photos of towering athletes who seem even more superhuman than they already are. Shooting at turf level makes your viewers think they're in the game. Knee pads are helpful, especially during long games or matches.

Shooting upwards toward the sports action often creates a unique photograph.

Shooting at a "Dutch angle," creates a photo that shows motion and speed.

Getting above the action is also an interesting way to capture sports. Get up high in the stands to shoot at least a few frames of the whole playing field. In some cases, you might even get a chance to shoot directly above the action.

Tilting your camera while shooting is called a "Dutch angle." It causes the horizon line to be crooked in the frame. In sports photography, it creates a sense of motion and speed.

LOOK FOR EMOTION

Human emotion is what makes sports so popular. Capturing that emotion with your photography is your main goal. Those are the kinds of images that make the front page of websites, newspapers, and magazine covers. Photographing action is wonderful, but capturing action plus emotion is a winning combination.

How do you find images with emotion? Look for celebrations on the field, either after a score or the final moments of the game. The best images fill the frame with the players' bodies or faces. Don't forget to look for emotion on the losing side, too, especially if the game was a hard-fought, crushing defeat.

Sports bring out great emotions on people's faces, both the players and the fans.

Sports fans give photographers a great opportunity to capture everything from excitement and joy to disappointment and frustration.

Another place to look for emotion is along the sidelines when the action gets tense. Fan reactions can also be priceless. In sports, emotion and drama is all around you. Be aware of the mood and point your camera in the right direction to capture that winning shot.

"Chimping" results in missed shots.

DON'T CHIMP

For digital camera owners, the ability to check photos right after you shoot is both a blessing and a curse. "Chimping" is when photographers get in the habit of peeking at their camera's LCD screen to see how their shots turned out. It's called chimping because when these photographers scroll to a good shot, they often make a noise like a chimpanzee: "Oooo-ooo-oo!"

Glancing at your camera's LCD screen is fine if you're checking exposure and sharpness. It's common to do this, especially when you first start shooting, or set up somewhere new on the field, or are using a different lens and exposure setting. Being able to make exposure adjustments as you shoot is one of digital photography's greatest strengths.

However, when you constantly chimp, it's very likely that you'll miss action on the field. Also, great shots can be captured when a play has just finished. You don't want to miss unexpected action, like a baseball runner stealing a base.

You might be very tempted to peek at your LCD screen, but try to resist looking at all your shots until the match is over. Not only will you potentially miss a shot, chimping can be dangerous, too. You might get bowled over by a linebacker when you have your head down checking your LCD.

By constantly checking the LCD screen on the back of your camera, you might miss unexpected action on the field.

PANNING TO SHOW MOTION

Sports photographers usually set their cameras so they can shoot with very fast shutter speeds. This freezes the action and makes time seem to stand still. However, there is another powerful way to create a sense of motion in a still photograph. It involves keeping the subject mostly in focus while the rest of the scene streaks across the frame in a blur.

This technique is called panning and it takes some practice. First, use a slower-than-normal shutter speed. With a telephoto lens and a fast-moving subject, you'll probably need a shutter speed between 1/30 and 1/60 second. For wide-angle lenses or slower-moving subjects, try starting at 1/4 second and work your way down.

As your subject moves past, aim your camera and follow along as you shoot. Because you're following the subject, it will remain mostly sharp. The rest of the scene will be moving as the image sensor is exposed to light. This causes the streaking effect that gives the illusion of motion. Be sure to use your camera's burst mode (continuous shooting) as you follow the subject to have the best chance of capturing a good frame.

SHOOTING DETAILS

Shooting exciting action is the most important job for sports photographers. However, don't overlook the details that make each sport unique. There is plenty of drama and interest off the field as well.

To complete your storytelling, be sure to turn around and take some photos of the fans. You will undoubtedly find some who are excited about their team and filled with emotion. Also take photos of the equipment used by the athletes. That includes close-ups of helmets, gloves, balls, nets, or other interesting items.

By the time you are done shooting a game or match, you should have a nice mix of action shots, crowd reactions, emotional athletes, and close-ups of items that add even more interest to your story.

A referee's whistle or a player's helmet are photographic details that add interest to your photo story.

CROPPING

Today's modern digital cameras shoot with such a high number of pixels that you can take just a part of the frame and create a totally new composition and it will still be high enough resolution to make prints or appear on a website.

Sports photographers usually try to fill the frame with action, or compose in a way that leaves no wasted space in the frame. In many cases, however, you'll have no choice but to crop afterwards. Subjects often move away from you just as the action peaks. And even when shooting with a big telephoto lens, a football player can look small in the viewfinder when he's on the other side of the field. In these cases, cropping is essential. With a high megapixel camera, you can crop the action tightly and still have a great picture.

Another reason to crop is for creative reasons. Sometimes a photo becomes a winner when distracting elements are cropped out. Don't be afraid to play with it. Professionals do this all the time. It's one way they get tight, well-composed action shots for publication.

With creative cropping, a cluttered team photo with many distracting elements becomes a dramatic action shot of a single soccer player.

A rock climber's hand makes an interesting cropped photo from the original shot.

THE DIGITAL DARKROOM

Photos taken with modern cameras are usually well exposed and in focus, but there's always room for improvement. That's where the digital darkroom comes in. Fixing a photo's range of tones (its light and dark pixels) can improve it dramatically. Color balance, sharpening, and cropping are also common enhancements. These are all easy to perform on modern digital photography software such as Photoshop, Lightroom, or GIMP. There are even inexpensive apps for cell phones that let you experiment with your photos.

Image editing software can be difficult to learn, but it is a fun way to improve your photos. Use the software's help menus, or search for online video instructions. Everyone was a beginner once, and many generous photographers are happy to share their skills.

Postproduction work can dramatically enhance a photo.

The left photo above is before image enhancement. In Photoshop, the first task was to fix the exposure and contrast. Yellow was added to counter the blue cast, common on cloudy days. Color vibrance was boosted, and then a vignette circled the image to draw the viewer's eye toward the center of the frame.

BACKING UP YOUR PHOTOS

Make copies of your digital images. Keep them safe on at least two storage devices. All hard drives will fail eventually. Without a backup, your photos will vanish, representing many months, perhaps years, of hard work.

In most professional studios, photos are backed up on several different devices. In addition to the hard drive on your main computer, use backup software every day to automatically copy all your photos onto a portable hard drive. These small devices get cheaper every year, with bigger capacities. Every few days or weeks, swap out the external drive with one that you might keep in a safe deposit box at your bank. This strategy is called having an off-site backup. If disaster strikes, such as your house burning down or washing away in a flood, your work will remain safe.

Portable hard drives hold a lot of photos and can be kept in different locations as off-site backups.

PORTABLE HARD DRIVE

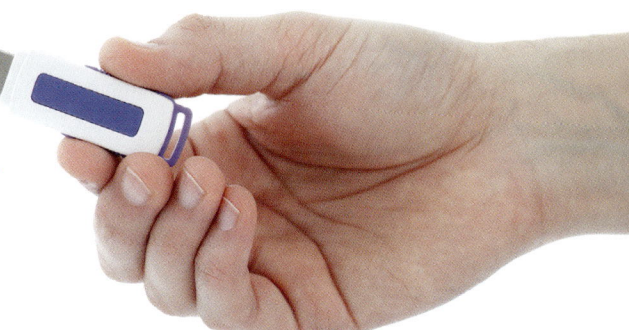

A USB flash drive is an easy and portable way to back up your photographs. It is a good device to use when traveling.

If you're just starting out, you don't need to rent a safe deposit box. Store your off-site backup at a friend or relative's house for safekeeping. You'll be glad you did if your files are ever damaged.

Some photographers store off-site backups in the Cloud. That means using the Internet to automatically store digital copies on large computer servers run by companies such as Dropbox, Apple, or Google. Cloud storage can be impractical because digital photo collections often grow to many gigabytes in size and could take days to upload. However, technology changes rapidly, and Cloud storage becomes more appealing with each passing year.

For extra protection, you can also keep your best files backed up on USB flash drives. After copying, toss them in a desk drawer. It's probably not totally necessary, but it'll give you peace of mind.

COPYRIGHT

Who owns your photos? You do, of course. The moment you press the shutter release button, you own the copyright to that image. To get even more protection, you can register your photos for a fee with the U.S. Copyright Office in Washington, DC, at copyright.gov. Registered or not, nobody has the right to use your images without your permission.

GLOSSARY

APERTURE
The opening in the lens that lets light pass through to the image sensor. The aperture is usually adjustable, and measured in f-stops.

CROPPING
Using image enhancement software in the digital darkroom to eliminate unwanted portions of an image, leaving only the most important part of the scene. Cropping is a powerful way to focus attention on your subject.

DEPTH OF FIELD
A range of distance (depth), from back to front, that is in sharp focus in your scene. A "shallow" depth of field has a very narrow range of sharp focus. It is seen most often with telephoto lenses when using large apertures (such as f/2.8), and is a useful technique for blurring distracting background clutter from your images.

DIGITAL NOISE
Noise is a collection of digital artifacts, which look like clumps of grains of sand that aren't really part of the scene. It occurs most often in low-light situations where the camera sensor is set with a high ISO number.

DIGITAL SINGLE LENS REFLEX (DSLR)
A digital single lens reflex camera is a kind of camera that features interchangeable lenses and sophisticated electronics. It captures images on a digital image sensor instead of film.

F-STOP
A number that is used to tell the size of a lens's opening, or aperture. Small numbers, such as f/2.8, represent a large aperture. Small apertures, which let in less light, include f/16 and f/22.

Image Sensor
The electronic device inside a digital camera that converts light into electronic signals, which are then processed and stored on a memory card.

ISO Number
A number that describes a camera sensor's sensitivity to light. Cameras that can shoot with high ISO numbers can capture images in very dim lighting conditions. The name ISO is the abbreviation for the International Organization for Standardization, a Swiss company. ISO is not an acronym for the company name. It is the root of the Greek word *isos*, which means "equal." It is pronounced "EYE-so."

Memory Card
After an image has been captured and processed by a digital camera, it is stored on a memory card, which is a solid-state storage device similar to a USB flash drive. Memory cards come in various speeds and storage capacities. Many can hold hundreds of images.

Sharpening
Although the human eye can detect lines of contrast in a scene with amazing sharpness, camera sensors are limited by the number of pixels they contain. This causes pictures to appear a little out of focus. Cameras and image editing software can "sharpen" images to make them appear almost as sharp as they seem to the eye.

ONLINE RESOURCES

To learn more about sports photography, visit abdobooklinks.com. These links are routinely monitored and updated to provide the most current information available.

INDEX

A
action camera 12, 13
angle of view 7, 16, 30
aperture 16, 18, 20, 21, 29
Apple 45
automatic (*see* program mode)

B
blur (*see also* camera shake) 18, 23, 24, 29, 36
burst mode 10, 27, 37

C
camera shake (*see also* blur) 18, 19, 22, 23, 24
cell phone camera 10, 42
chimping 34, 35
close-ups 38
Cloud 45
color balance 42
composition 20, 28, 29, 40
continuous shooting mode (*see* burst mode)
copyright 45
Copyright Office, U.S. 45
crop 8, 40, 42

D
depth of field 10, 15, 21
digital camera 6, 11, 34, 40
digital darkroom 42
digital noise 8, 18, 24
digital photography 6, 42
Dropbox 45
DSLR (Digital Single Lens Reflex) camera 7, 8, 9, 10, 11, 13, 20, 24
Dutch angle 31

E
Eastman Kodak 6
exposure 8, 10, 18, 20, 23, 34, 42

F
field of view 14
fill the frame 28, 32, 40
film 6
filter 9, 15
fisheye lens 14
fixed lens 11
focal length 17, 23
focus 10, 15, 20, 21, 26, 36, 42
frames per second (fps) 27
f-stop 20, 21

G
Garmin 13
GIMP 42
Google 45
GoPro 13

H
handhold 22, 23, 25
hard drive 44

I
image processor 8
image sensor 6, 8, 14, 18, 19, 23, 24, 37
image stabilization 24
Internet 45
ISO 18, 24

L
LCD screen 34, 35
lens 6, 7, 10, 11, 14, 15, 16, 17, 20, 22, 23, 24, 25, 29, 34
lens filter 15
lens hood 17
Lightroom 42

M
megapixel 8, 40
memory card 6
mirrorless camera 11
monopod 25

O
off-site backup 44, 45
Olympus 13

P
panning 36
Photoshop 42
pixel 8, 40, 42
program mode ("P") 20, 23

R
resolution 8, 40
rule of thirds 29

S
sensor 8, 24
sharpness 7, 15, 23, 34, 42
shutter 8, 19, 23
shutter release button 8, 27, 45
shutter speed 10, 18, 19, 20, 23, 24, 36
skylight filter 9
Sony 13
Sun 9, 17
super-wide lens 14

T
teleconverter 17
telephoto lens 10, 14, 16, 17, 22, 23, 25, 36, 40
telephoto zoom lens 16
tones 42
tripod 22, 25

U
USB drive 45
UV filter 9, 15

V
vibration reduction (VR) 24, 25
viewfinder 8, 22, 26, 28, 29, 40

W
Washington, DC 45
wide-angle lens 10, 13, 14, 15, 19, 23, 25, 36

Z
zoom lens 16